Sta

BOOK 1:
Children and Beginners

By Valerian Ruminski

ISBN: 1542720443
ISBN-13:9781542720441

DEDICATION

This book is dedicated to all of my musical 'fathers' that have taught me since my real father died when I was 10 years old. Joe Mankowski, Anthony Furnivall, Frank Scinta, Tynan Jones, Gary Burgess, Louis Quilico, Christofer Macatsoris, Bill Schuman and Seth Riggs. Each one of them contributed some part to my vocal and mental development as a singer.

STARTING TO SING BOOK 1

CONTENTS

ACKNOWLEDGMENTS

I would like to acknowledge all my educators in the musical field, all the companies that have seen fit to hire me to perform over the years and all those in my close circle who have helped me produce my books including Eileen Breen and Dan Patterson who offer sound advice and logical editing.

Prologue

I began singing at a very young age. I remember singing and I remember music more than anything else from my earliest memories. I remember hearing music on the radio and listening to it from records. It was a mishmosh of many different types and styles of music. I remember the song 'Raindrops Keep Falling on My Head' by Burt Bacharach vividly. The melody captured my attention.

I was music aware at a very young age. Hopefully, your child is too. If they show signs of wanting to hear music, sing music or dance to music then it should be nurtured and encouraged.

At 5 or 6 years old I was singing all the time. I sang silly songs that I heard on a record player my father had put in my bedroom. I listened to everything in his record collection. Jazz, classical, symphonic, marching bands, crooners and more. I was open to all types of music and I began trying to mimic singing that I heard. The first step in singing is to be a mimic. We copy what we hear and then we refine it. We fake it till we make it.

Usually, from my experience, most children do not know what they are doing when they sing. They simply sing. They open their mouths and let sound come out. They do not understand where the sound is coming from or how it is made or what the right or wrong process is to sing. They just sing and that's alright....for awhile.

Opening your mouth and letting sound come out is a healthy, emboldening exercise and it is good when children do this. But, after a time, if they are serious about singing well, they need to learn some basic rules and knowledge about what they are attempting to do with their voices. That is where I come in.

I have a lot of experience with singing. I sang as a small child, I was accepted into a prestigious Episcopal choir at 7 years old, I sang in a wonderful high school chorus and I made my Metropolitan Opera debut at the age of 32.

I see bad and wrong things every day with young singers and even veteran singers who have been singing for years. Sometimes it is very sad to see how some people hurt themselves and do the wrong things when they sing. It could be so much simpler and easier.

Another issue is the people around the singers and the jealousy, the misunderstanding and the socio-political motivations for preventing a child or young person from singing or learning to sing correctly. I will discuss this in depth later.

There is a way to sing correctly. There is a way of thinking about singing that is better than some other ways. There is a science and a system which is part of what singing is all about and these components need to be known and studied by singers of all types and ages. I will show you those components in this book.

This book exists to get you started in your goal of getting your child or yourself to sing without falling into the pitfalls and dangers of incorrect singing or misleading mentors and teachers who do not know what they are doing. There are more charlatans teaching voice than there are Walmarts in your town. We all need to be aware of this and act accordingly.

So take your time and read this first volume of books designed to help kids, teenagers and adults to sing better and healthier and if it helps you then read the next one. We should always be learning and growing.

Chapter 1

Air Converters

When we sing we are all converting air into sound. Air brought into our lungs which is used to make sound is expelled in a different way than air used to simply breath.

Think of a balloon. We blow air into the balloon and then, if we do not pinch or hold shut the opening, the air blows out immediately without a sound except for a whoosh. If we expiate air without holding it back somehow we are acting much like the balloon. Air in, air out. Air only. No sound (other than the sound of the air going in and out).

Now if we make the effort to hold the air back we can do that in one of two ways. We can either simply hold our breath still with no movement one way or the other or we can release the air more slowly by 'phonating' or bringing our vocal cords together to make a sound. This, using our balloon again, is like pinching the opening shut and allowing the balloon to whine and shriek with sound because the air is vibrating the tight rubber edges of the aperature as we pull it shut. The air wants to escape but we force it to escape slowly which results in sound. Our voices do the same thing.

I could spend an entire book describing the mechanism of the vocal cords and the physical structure of it but that will do little to help you become a good singer. The voice is inside your throat. It is invisible to you as you use it. So you must learn how to operate it blindly in order to become a truly facile singer with good technique. If you are all caught up in the technical aspects of how the cords are working and frozen by analysis paralysis then your singing will suffer for it.

All you need to know is that the vocal cords are made of specialized flesh (in the same way your heart or liver have different kinds of flesh that are specialized to do a specific job) and that specialized flesh performs the work of vibrating to make sound in your throat for all the years you are alive.

These cords can be injured by improper use or bad nutrition or abuse just like any other part of your body. The cords are not impervious to pain or abuse. They can form nodes which are like callouses. The cords can be coated with different types of phlegm and perform less well than usual. Your cords are an amazing, complex and responsive system of nerves and flesh and cartilage which can be trained to do unbelievable feats of acoustic gymnastics. Or not.

Beyond that the working of the cords is dependant upon much of the rest of the body. The way you breath, the way you stand, the way your diaphragm is used and the unique connection between your brain and your cords are all parts of what allows you to be able to sing. Whether you sing well or poorly is the question.

The hardest aspect of teaching singing is when you must force a student to recognize that something about the mechanisms at work in their body prevents them from being able to sing well and with a pleasant tone. The sad truth is that not everyone was meant to sing. This is not to say that someone should be prevented from singing but, as far as making a living and singing professionally, not everyone possesses a singing voice that people want to hear or will enjoy hearing.

It would be very easy for a teacher to lie to a student and tell them they will be famous one day in order to take their money for lessons. Many teachers do this. It is reprehensible. At some point an honest teacher must tell a student that they can continue studying to sing but, in the teachers opinion, they will never sing professionally.

This can be a very emotional moment for some singers. Some want to believe that hard work and study will make them able to sing like any other great singer. This is not true. Singing is not like being an accountant or an architect. In those professions if you follow the numbers and apply the mathematics you will succeed. You may do so without a natural talent for accounting or architecture. But achieving success singing cannot occur without natural talent.

Why, you may ask?

I suppose that for some beauty may be in the eye of the beholder and that there are singers with 'ugly' voices that do appeal to an audience. Bad sounds, improper technique and odd resonances from certain singers do make their voices somewhat palatable. Take for instance Joe Cocker, Tom Waits, Seal (who sings with a rasp) and Bob Dylan. These singers could be used to counter my argument. I concede that there are exceptions to any rule but, by and large, there are limits to the extremes of vocal production which still make it true that not everyone can have a professional singing voice.

If you are one of the unfortunate people that simply cannot make your voice do what it needs to do in order to be enjoyed by an audience I hope that your teacher is honest enough to tell you so that you can pursue some other career. Of course you can always sing as a hobby. Being honest with a singer is an act of mercy which can save some people decades of wasted time, effort and emotions.

I knew a man who was convinced that he could sing. He was very bright and intelligent and even had a PhD in physics. He lectured in physics at a University but he auditioned for the voice department. At the age of 54 he was accepted into the department because he got a 100 score on the written music test. His audition though was a joke.

I actually was present as he sang this audition. The technique, the tone, the resonance and his pronunciation were all horribly bad. He had studied and worked very hard but his voice, at the age of 54, was no more pleasing or artful than it had ever been. He simply could not sing.

His dream was to go to europe and audition for opera houses as a tenor. He actually had tried this before and during the intervening years his efforts had caused his marriage to break apart twice. Now he was auditioning again and causing the same tensions to resurface. He eventually divorced his wife for a third time.

I recount this story to show you that passions can run high and that no one should discount the power of a dream. But sometimes dreams do not come true no matter how hard you work. You cannot fit a size 12 foot into a size 7 shoe and you cannot make the facial structure and resonance chambers of a face and a body change.

But, if you are lucky enough to have the basic raw materials to generate a pleasing tone when you sing then the door is open for you to work hard and to try to succeed in a business which is unforgiving, relentlessly hard, mostly confusing and always less than rewarding financially. Make no mistake...those people who make millions singing are 1 in 1,000,000.

Returning to our discussion of air converting there is no simpler way to explain the physical act of singing than describing it as converting air into sound. In truth that is all that it is.

Some aspects of converting air into sound are the control of the air, the compression of the air and the measuring of the release of the air. Isn't that simple?

Of course none of it is simple or else everyone would be a wonderful singer. Layering these tasks one over the other makes it very complicated to sing correctly. So why do some children seem to do things naturally without any instruction to create beautiful singing voices? It happens. But I would warn such people to beware of believing that singing with ease at 7 years old will be a permanent state. That is a trap that many children fall into.

Singers are wonderful mimics. Like a parrot a child can mimic a sound or a voice. Sometimes they can mimic a singing voice so perfectly that we are fooled into thinking that they are 'naturally' good singers. But there is a wall that divides a great mimic from a great singer. That wall is called 'hard work'.

When adults mimic singing they create what is

called an 'affected' sound which means a sort of false resonance. Think of someone trying to mimic the voice of Yoda from Star Wars. Most people can do it with laryngeal compression. They create vocal tension which squashes their natural resonance and thus they sound like a cartoon character.

Some people 'mimic' opera singing by belting out a loud tone coupled with laryngeal compression which results in an exaggerated representation of what they think an opera singer sounds like. Most of the time this type of mimicked opera singing sounds quite ugly. Great opera singers do not sound ugly.

One way or the other the effect is the same. Children mimic a sound and then perfect the mimicking. They do not perfect the singing voice. If you notice the mimicking that they do is of a particular song which is sung by a particular singer in a particular way. If you ask the same child to sing a song without mimicking a singer or a song that they know they are clueless and unable to produce a pleasing tone or to navigate the difficulties of high notes and a melody which they are not familiar with.

These children are what I call 'one trick ponies'. They can only sing what they hear on the radio or from a CD by repeating the song over and over again. They have no knowledge of how high the song is or how low the tones might go. If they sing the song on a Monday and start on a C (purely at random) they wonder why, when the next day comes, they have a hard time singing the same song because they started singing it on a D or an E and because they had no idea what the difference is.

I am discussing this type of mimicking in order to

illustrate that a 'natural talent' is rare. Eventually everyone must take the time to actually study singing, sing scales and concentrate on the voice in order to succeed in the business of singing. There is rarely a shortcut to great singing.

Being an air converter means that you must play with the air. A singer must have a very comfortable relationship with the manipulation of the air in their body as it passes in and out of the lungs and through the cords.

The first thing to think about is that in order to play with air you must have some to play with. This means taking deep breaths. No one ever got famous singing by breathing in a shallow manner (other than maybe Bob Dylan). In order to produce large long tones you must take large and deep breaths.

A glass is filled from the bottom up. You can't pour liquid into a glass starting halfway up. It automatically goes to the bottom. But, unfortunately, breathing does not work this way. It is possible to breath 'from the middle of the glass' or even from the top. The higher up you breath the more shallow your breaths are. As a singer you must consciously decide and work to fill the glass from the bottom up. Deep breath. Low breath. Of course the lower the breath goes the more you will eventually be able to fill the lungs with. If you fill the glass from the middle up that is only a half glass full of liquid.

So start by breathing, not singing. Singing is much more complicated than breathing. Let's start simply. You take a deep breath and feel how low it goes. Let it go deep and then hold it. Feel what holding the air back does.

Continue to hold it. Then release it fully. No singing.

The next breath do the same, deeply. When you feel ready and that you have repeated this deep breathing enough then you can bring your voice into play. Allow the cords to slowly come together. Your voice will produce a sound...not singing but a very primal UHHH. Feel the creation of this simplest of sounds. This is what I call the Moment of Conception.

We will continue with exercises and observations as we move forward in Starting to Sing 1. For now let us discuss more about the basics of singing and the responsibilities of being a singer.

Chapter 2

Starting to Start

So you have a child that is singing. This can be good or bad depending on how you approach it and what you want to happen. Maybe you are a parent that doesn't want your child to sing because you are afraid of a career for your child that you know nothing about and do not understand. That is normal. But, in the end, this is about what your child wants and needs.

I have seen parents play a sad and dangerous game with their children over this decision. The worst way of handling it is to dangle the possibility of supporting them as they begin to succeed in singing and then pulling that support away when the parents realize that it is actually starting to happen. At first they allow the child to take voice lessons and sing under the guidance of a professional. Then, as the lessons start to show that they are good and proficient at singing, opportunities begin to arise for competitions and recitals and concerts which the parents balk at and deny the child permission to participate in.

Since many of these children are under the age of 18 they cannot decide on their own to continue to study, they cannot jump on a bus or a train and go to New York City to compete, and they cannot pay for lessons on their own without a job when the parents pull back their financing of this endeavour.

So, what is created is a situation of tension and anger when a child wants to do something and has been encouraged to do something that, in the end, does not fit into the plans of the parents.

This undoubtedly occurs for many activities other than singing. Acting, certain sports, joining the military and other semi-dangerous professions sometimes repel parents from aiding in the pursuit of a child's dream.

I strongly advise parents to think about what they are doing. Sit down and explain to the child that this is a commitment and that they have to be serious about it. But, by the same token, the parents have to be serious about it as well and agree that if things go well and the child wants to pursue this vocation that the parents are 100% behind them and will help them as much as they can.

On the flipside I have seen the opposite happen and it is just as heartbreaking. Sometimes children pursue singing and the parents are totally oblivious to it. They don't care one way or the other and they don't participate or attend or financially support the efforts of the child. Even when the child has great potential and the parents are informed that with a little help something wonderful could happen certain parents turn a deaf ear and offer nothing. Their ambivalence and disinterest probably runs deeper than simply supporting a singing career. I have seen singers that, when push comes to shove and it is time for the parents to buy a plane ticket or invest in a musical instrument, are left out in the cold and high and dry.

Another type of parent is equally destructive and that is the 'stage parent' syndrome. Beware this mindset! There are parents who believe that their child is the greatest, best and most talented and deserving child on the planet. They are awesome even if nobody else sees it or agrees. These parents will knock down doors and walls to get their child heard and if they hear a negative assessment of their child's ability they will simply disregard that person as a hack and find someone else to tell them how phenomenal their kid is. Please, don't do this.

As we discussed in the last chapter sometimes a child just doesn't have it. They are not good enough. Eventually this will become evident and it must be acknowledged. Continuing to hammer away trying to create interest and success without the proper ingredients is a fool's errand. Worse still is the situation where the child realizes that they are not all that good and they begin to feel embarrassed that their parents are pushing them out onto the stage to humiliate them because they haven't been able to deal with the fact that their child is not the next musical Einstein. See the film Citizen Kane for perspective on this.

So decide now, if you are reading this book, how far you are willing to go. Don't start and then get cold feet later when your kid is ready to fly to NYC and sing in a competition and don't push them when it becomes clear they aren't cut out for it.

The saddest and most difficult part of the journey for a young singer, and even older singers, is who to trust. This is an issue that is universal in the singing world. There are many people out there that simply do not know what the heck they are talking about. That would be okay if it weren't damaging to the voice and psyche of a young singer.

You will see ads in magazines and newspapers for voice teachers and people who give 'Master Classes' to young singers. There is no doubt that many of these people are qualified and well intentioned. But, sadly, many of them are ignorant dabblers who know 1% of something and try to spin it into a career. Some of them are singers who just graduated from college who think they know something but oftentimes know only the most basic and rudimentary fundamentals of the voice and have not been out into the world to see how things really are. Some of these people are plain old heartless opportunists who are looking for pawns to make money off of and don't give a damn what happens to a voice they ruin. It is hard to differentiate the good from the bad but at least I am warning you.

So, where can you go for honesty? Well, even though I am selling a book, I believe I am honest and genuine in my efforts to help you find the right path. This book should be a compass. Beyond that I would seek out the most professional people. Don't ask your local church organist or some old lady who had a career singing in a community choir. Seek out someone at a University or an institution known for producing quality singers or, if you know someone, seek out a parent with a child who is singing well and ask them for direction.

So we have discussed the most basic mechanisms of starting to sing and we have discussed the nature of parental support in singing for children and the landscape of teachers for singing. This is a complicated vocation and we will touch on these topics over and over again as we proceed.

One of the more interesting and confusing aspects of singing is what to sing. In the 21st Century there are so many choices of what to sing that it can be mind boggling to a beginner. These choices lead to the question of what type of singer a child wants to be. Most people gravitate to what they know and most children know the pop music that is on their computers and iPods and Mp3 players. It is not surprising that most kids want to sing the songs that they hear by Justin Bieber and Beyonce' and Adele. But are these legitimate singing goals for a beginner?

Unfortunately the technique that facilitates the best singing in any category is the classical technique which children are exposed to the least. Thus most kids stumble into singing by listening to poor singing techniques and copying them. That is not a great way to succeed.

I am not suggesting that every child needs to learn to sing a Mozart aria before they can sing a Justin Bieber song. Not at all. But, I am saying that the techniques involved in building a 'classical voice' are the very same techniques that will make a child singer strong, capable, flexible and long lasting. Those are things that are very desirable.

Going back to the basic techniques that I mentioned earlier it is vital for a new singer to 1. Feel the breath and the voice 2. Have a knowledge of what their high note is and their lowest note 3. Doing vocal exercises where they spend time navigating the terrain of the voice and getting used to how it works and 4. Separating the singing of words and melodies from singing 'core exercises' which strengthen the voice.

When an athlete plays a sport they do not play the sport to strengthen themselves and build muscles. They lift weights for that. Then, after lifting weights, they go out on the field and use the muscles they have built to play the sport and succeed. In the same way a singer does not strengthen or tone the voice by simply singing. A singer builds the voice with vocal exercises which expose flaws in the singing technique which the singer must fix in order to sing better.

Lifting weights is a monotonous, repetitive exercise and so should be singing 'vocalises' as they are called. Long chains of monosyllabic words sung to repetitive and difficult melodies will test the limits of a voice and reveal whatever flaws are there to reveal.

There is an eastern mentality in art and other disciplines that espouses that making a mistake is forbidden and a horrible, shameful thing. Students flagellate themselves because, during a lesson with a teacher, they tragically sang the wrong note or the wrong vowel or, God forbid, they cracked a note or flubbed a line! This is a very destructive and counter-productive approach to music teaching and the performing discipline.

Think of it. If one is always afraid of making a mistake then the odds are high they will make one. If I am spending all my time avoiding the issue that is making my voice crack because I don't ever want it to crack then how will I ever remedy the problem? One must crack and continue to crack until they figure out how to stop cracking.

One of my voice teachers told me a story. A young

couple brought their daughter to a renowned figure skating coach to ask if he would coach their daughter who was highly proficient in figure skating. The old coach was retired and he told them no. He was finished coaching. But the parents persisted and when pushed the old coach told them he would work with the young girl on one condition...when he told her to fall down she was to fall down on the ice without hesitation. The parents agreed and the training began.

The girl came to practice and the coach told her that when he clapped his hands together twice she was to stop skating and fall down. She thought this was an odd rule but she obeyed him.

Time after time, during a good run where she was skating flawlessly, he would clap his hands and she would fall. Over and over again this happened and eventually the girl got very frustrated and tired of falling. She complained to her parents that he was breaking her rhythm and that she wanted to finish a routine but he consistently stopped her by clapping his hands and making her fall.

Finally, after many months, she was entered into a competition and the old coach and her parents took her to the auditorium and let her loose. This was the first time that the coach could not clap his hands and make her fall. She was so happy and emboldened by the fact that she would not be forced to fall that she easily skated the course and never fell once. She earned a prize medal.

This story illustrates that making mistakes in front of someone who understands how growth happens is alright and will result in a stronger and more confident student. One has to 'get out the cracks' in front of the teacher so that the cracks do not appear when one is making a Carnegie Hall debut!

So now we return to the question of what type of singing a child embraces. I was frequently brought sheet music (from students that were informed that such things were needed and that we did not just pull music out of the air or sing to a CD) of songs that were totally inappropriate for a new singer to sing. They brought me modern pop songs that were stylistically crafted for the particular voice and sound of a famous pop singer. One does not learn how to sing by trying to mimic Michael Jackson or Bono or Sting or The Red Hot Chili Peppers. Trying to sing songs that have no melody or punctuated rhythms without the need for breath control or use of the diaphragm do nothing to create a good singer.

In the end the children who come to a voice lesson who want me to teach them to sing 'I'm Happy' by Pharrell Williams are doing themselves no good and are wasting my time. The song asks nothing, shows nothing and accomplishes nothing for the new singer. It is like asking a world class chef to make you a hot dog. Nothing to see here.

We can get into the whole issue of repertoire and modern music and melody and all that but in the end a song must be singable by everyone and not just the one person who recorded it. I mean, who wants to hear anyone but Michael Jackson sing Beat It or Billie Jean? Who cares to hear another singer perform 'Hello' by Adele? These are songs that are meant to be performed by one person and one person only. The voice is unique, the production is unique and the style of singing these particular lyrics are highly stylized and particular to the singer.

If you take a song like 'Somewhere Over The Rainbow' from the Wizard of Oz by Harold Arlen now you have something to work with. It is a song that ANYONE can sing. Even though Judy Garland immortalized it the song is still something that is universally adaptable for any singer. The melody is an obstacle course for the voice with high notes and low notes and a sense of line and breath. There are thousands of songs like that for a singer to sing. Singing songs like that reveal the true sound of the singer, a unique sound which identifies them as themselves and not some mimic trying to sound like Michael Jackson or Adele.

I discourage young singers from choosing songs which are pop fluff and without technical merit because it is the best choice for them. Singing a song by Beyonce' does nothing to help them technically and will only get people to compare them to Beyonce' and comparing them to Beyonce' will most oftentimes make them the vocal loser.

So, your child wants to be a pop star and I don't want them singing frivolous pop songs. How can that work? Well, it can.

The first step towards getting your child to sing is to encourage them. Sometimes you don't even need to do that. They will sing on their own with no prodding. This is a very good sign that they have the desire to sing. Without the desire there will be no career.

Once they have started to sing in the shower or in their bedroom or on the school bus or in the mall then the process has begun. Playing with their voice is the best way for them to get a handle on it. During this time a raw, unshaped and basic singing voice will emerge. Once this happens you can begin to do small things to help them and support the growth of that voice.

You can encourage them to join a local choir or to take voice lessons. You can buy them CD's of music that will provide them with a broad background of the many types of music they may want to sing including jazz, classical and pop. You can also refrain from giving your uneducated opinion of what you are hearing them do as they stumble and make mistakes with their singing. You can keep yourself from criticizing what you hear and you can choose not to tell them that they sing badly and should not try to sing. At this phase they simply need positive feedback.

If your child shows a great ability and is singing all the time then it might be wise to think about getting them a voice teacher. If you go this route, choose wisely. Do not just go to the first person that pops up. Do a little research and ask around. Go and ask for advice from someone in a position of musical prominence in your area like the director of the local symphony or a choral director or the music director of a notable church that performs classical standards by the great composers and not just hymns.

Most children do not start out as soloists. They start by being part of a group and singing with other children. After doing that for a time, if they are exceptional, they stand out and it becomes obvious that they have the ability and talent to sing on their own. Time will reveal this.

When that happens find a voice teacher and get them started taking one on one lessons possibly twice a month or more. These lessons should be simple and the child should not be burdened with many difficult songs to sing. If your child is memorizing pop songs right away, without doing basic vocal exercises, then you have chosen the wrong voice teacher.

The goal of the teacher you choose should be getting the child to sing properly and in a healthy way. Their goal should not be getting them to register for voice competitions by learning popular rock songs. Competitions will come down the road once the hard work of basic vocalise technique has been initiated and implemented. Throwing a child on Young Apprentice after a few months of getting them to mimic an Adele song is not the way to establish a solid foundation for a lifetime of singing.

As a parent, if you are supportive of your child being a singer, you may see winning a competition as the best way to fulfill their needs. This is not always the case. Achieving too much too soon without the proper foundation can lead to ruin and the destruction of the voice within a few short years.

Many young child singing stars lose or permanently damage their voices fairly quickly after gaining some notoriety and being asked to record songs and sing on tour with a microphone. They are pushed into a position of using the voice in an industrial manner for which they are ill prepared. Without the steady building of solid technique the voice will shrivel and wilt under the pressure of constant use and abuse.

Navigating certain notes and words of certain difficult passages in a song will ravage the cords and eventually damage them. The child may start getting laryngitis and the voice may seize up and stop working for periods of time forcing the child to cancel concerts and go on vocal rest for days or weeks. This is a sure sign of vocal distress and improper singing technique and if the warning signs are not heeded the voice may lose it's ability to produce a pleasing tone permanently.

But, as we see so often, the pursuit of fame and fortune can seduce a family into going 'all in' on the most fleeting type of vocal preparation. Parents see dollar signs when the raw, primal beauty of their child's voice can be prostituted to the pop industry and turned into a product. No thought is given to the fragile instrument which is laying the golden egg and without prudent care and guidance it can be lost forever.

Once a child finds an audience and starts to become popular the money will come. With the money will come handlers and marketers and recording contracts and companies and individuals who do not care about the health and well being of the child. They only care about dollar signs. Because of that they vigorously guard their golden goose and do whatever is necessary to make that goose sing and sing and sing. Voice teachers are closely monitored to prevent them from altering the 'marketable sound' of their child prodigy and no deviation from whatever misguided technique has taken root will be allowed.

What I am describing happens to only a fraction of the children who enter the singing profession. The 'lucky ones'. But it is a cage with golden bars. If a parent is not careful they can push their child down a road of financial prosperity and vocal ruin. If a parent pays heed to my warnings they will deal with both sides of the situation and make sure that the voice that is producing these fortunes is well taken care of and properly used.

Chapter 3

Who's To Judge?

One of the most understandable actions many parents take in trying to assess the potential of their child's singing voice is to turn to the most obvious 'authority' for answers and advice. To many this becomes the motley crew on television shows like 'The Voice' or 'America's Got Talent' or 'American Idol' or one of one hundred other television shows that present adults with scant vocal experience passing judgement and ordaining who can sing and who cannot sing on a week to week basis.

Let me state this as clearly as possible: Just because a person has attained fame and fortune with a hit song or a hit album or a string of hit albums it does not make them an authority on who can sing, how to sing or who should make a career singing. It gives them no right to dispense technical advice to a novice. Just because they are famous is no indication that they possess the knowledge necessary to turn someone else into a hit singer. They themselves may have a few tricks to produce a singing voice which other people want to spend money to hear but that does not mean they know how to groom proper technique in a singer. They may be smart enough to be able to tell the difference between someone with obvious talent and someone who obviously sounds unsaleable but that small ability is not enough to qualify them to be a judge with the awesome responsibility being a judge entails.

I am amused and partly horrified when I turn the

station and come upon a young child singing under the bright lights in front of a full audience being judged by a spray tanned rock star, a scantily clad female pop vocalist or someone who has spent their lives using studio techniques and microphones to create the illusion of having a groomed pop singing voice. It is a sad joke and a disservice to the contestants who stand in line for days to get the chance to be subjected to ill informed 'experts' who could neither build a voice in a student nor fix a voice if it were put in front of them to fix.

To be fair some of these judges have knowledge and experience with vocal lessons and exercises and technique but, from what I have seen, that is few and far between. More likely these are celebrity pop and rock singers who have been riding on abusive vocal techniques for their entire career without even knowing the difference. They have no vocal regimen, they have no exercises and they do not possess the ability to understand what they are doing with their voices either during a recording or when they sing live onstage in front of an audience with a band. They are mostly as much in the dark about their voices and what proper vocal maintenance requires as any regular person in the street.

The only difference between a famous pop singer with no guidance or training and a child who starts singing with no guidance or training is that the famous pop singer has some natural talent that they have pushed into the limelight and have capitalized on. Just because they have signed a multi-million dollar contract does not mean that they possess some kind of secret knowledge about the voice and singing that they can impart on a few lucky up and coming talents.

It may seem to make sense that a pop singer must be well trained and knowledgeable about their instrument or else they would not become famous but, strangely enough, that is not the case. The highways of pop music fame are littered with singers that have blown out, damaged and destroyed their voices. That is the reason I am writing this book. I am trying to put out the warning signal to parents and children everywhere that you can damage the voice permanently by singing incorrectly and that it is not easy to know when the voice is being damaged and that by the time it is severely damaged it may be too late for you to fix it. I am warning you, the parents and singers out there, that there is a wrong way and a right way to sing and that singing the right way does not mean singing opera. It means that you can sing pop and rock and jazz and Broadway and classical music correctly with a bit of effort being mindful of your vocal health and that you will be glad you did.

Most people like the judges on these television shows only recognize the raw and natural talent of the kids that they hear. They pay no mind to vocal health or technique or vocal exercises. They basically believe that you are either a prodigy that comes out fully formed or you are not meant to sing. This discounts the thousands of children who have gone from no experience or discipline with singing to people with major singing careers. You can sound sloppy and raw and unmarketable one year and then, after practice and guidance, you can go on to singing on stage and having a hit record four years later. But, after one hearing, these geniuses with golden toilets and an entourage will discount you and put you out to pasture. There is a better way.

The job of the judges on 'American Idol' or 'The Voice' is to find the flavor of the day. They want to find some kid who is like a very ripe strawberry that they can pick off the vine and sell right to a contract so that pop music producers can put them into a studio and build catchy pop songs around them. The pop music industry is like any other industry. They need product. They are not going to sit around and wait for the new Prince or Bruce Springsteen to emerge somewhere in Nebraska at a whiskey bar. They will work hard to create a product around the newest pretty face and serviceable voice to come along. There is a huge pre-teen and teenage market worth billions of dollars and that machine must be fed. If you want your child to become the latest victim of the system as a primped, produced and vocally compromised singer then go for it. I am simply here to tell you that you run the odds of having a child with a ruined voice within a few very short years. If that is worth a few million dollars to you then that is your choice.

What I am saying is that you could possibly have both worlds. If you pay mind to have your child instructed properly as well as pursuing pop fame and fortune then they might stand a chance of having some longevity.

You may wish to ask me why I believe these famous judges are not the authority that everyone thinks they are. As I said, some of them have sufficient knowledge to give tips and pointers and maybe even a voice lesson of some kind. But, from what I have seen, most of them do not posses the type of knowledge necessary to cultivate a singer or to help a singer through vocal distress because of improper singing techniques.

Many of these judges and people who become famous in the pop music business as singers do so by quirks of fate and spur of the moment situations which thrust them into the public eye. They go from singing in church or at grammar school to singing industrially every night at stadiums and on television. They go from being heard by a few hundred people to being heard by millions. This happens almost overnight. Many of them are not ready for what is happening and they certainly are not equipped to know what they must do to prevent the voice from being damaged by abuse.

Michael Jackson, despite his fame and experience, had a voice that was in decline. His voice was abused over many years and his handlers did not want him to change anything about the way that he sang in order to relieve the stress. They were worried that he would lose millions by altering the way he sang. I have heard tapes of old voice lessons of Michael Jackson. I know people who used to teach him. The sounds I heard were not pretty. If you watch video of his appearances in the few years before he died you will notice his fist covering his mouth as he grasps the tiny microphone in front of his face. Why would you cover the entire microphone if you want your voice to be heard live? He clearly didn't.

Julie Andrews, at a more advanced age, had an operation to try to fix her voice which made it much worse. She has since retired from singing. Adele, it is rumored, has also been having some issues with vocal distress and may have already had a procedure performed which could alter her voice for the rest of her life.

The pop music life makes demands on the vocal mechanism which are daily, industrial and chronic. If approached with intelligence and care these demands can be managed and the voice may be spared of pain and treatments.

Chapter 4

What's the Difference?

As we discuss singing, no matter if it's a child or an adult, we inevitably must discuss the various types of singing in order to deal with the vocal technique and fix problems that are uniquely associated with the type of singing that someone is doing.

There are many categories of singing types including pop, rock, heavy metal, punk, rap, jazz, Broadway and, of course, classical which can also be subdivided into a few categories.

Of all of the types of singing that exist perhaps the most destructive and technically misunderstood category is Broadway. If you are a young person going into singing songs in a Broadway style you are opening yourself up to the greatest possibility of vocal damage. This is because Broadway singing is the perfect storm which combines the need for volume with the deadly 'forward' brightness which is so destructive to the vocal apparatus and is so strongly identified with the Broadway style of singing.

Pop and rock and metal are actually not as taxing on the voice as Broadway. This is because most pop and rock and metal singers sing within the range they are able to sing in. They are writing their own songs and they are not making themselves sing high notes and difficult vowel and consonant combinations if they don't want to. Some do and it hurts them. But, by and large, most of these pop, rock and metal singers are singing in their comfort zones. Eventually, after touring and singing day after day, they too damage their voices. But the easiest way to quickly damage your voice is to sing Broadway.

Why? Well, Broadway forces a singer who may not have the proper technique to sing notes that they themselves did not write. They are forced to sing the music of other composers who, very frequently, have no idea how to write for singers. They do not know what the voice categories are. They do not know the difference between a soprano and a mezzo-soprano or a tenor and a baritone or a bass. They simply write and expect a singer to sing it. They also frequently do not have any idea about the proper vowels to put on high notes. Some vowels work much better and aid in good vocal technique when they are placed on high notes. Some are quite bad. Many of the composers do not know the difference.

Add to that the need for these Broadway singers to produce volume. In pop, rock and metal the singers use a microphone in the studio and on stage. Even though Broadway singers also sing with microphones they still must produce more volume than a pop singer because of the nature of the music they are singing and because of the expectations of the audience with a particular type of sound. Many times there are long held straight tones in Broadway singing which you do not hear in pop, rock or metal. This, if done correctly, can be sung without trauma. But, many times, Broadway singers belt out a note or an entire song in a manner which, invisibly inside their throat, is causing the vocal mechanism to seize and revolt.

Actually the technique has been named 'The Belt'

and it is one of the most abhorrent and damaging trends in the history of singing. If you are sending your child off to begin a career in singing Broadway music you need to be very careful and make sure that they understand what they are doing and how they can possibly mitigate the damage with some techniques that can shield them from the damage of 'The Belt'.

Vocal damage is taken quite too lightly in our culture. People seem to think that the voice is some rock hard or steel mechanism that can withstand any type of abuse even screaming and yelling and shouting. The vocal mechanism is much more fragile than people think and permanent damage can occur in a relatively short amount of time. Sleep and drinking water and remaining aware of when you are pushing the voice too far can help prevent vocal trouble but when money is on the line many singers will push the voice like whipping a carriage horse in Central Park. Eventually the horse collapses.

I would have to give you audio examples of the type of bad singing that Broadway belting can produce. Some of it may sound pleasing to the ear because it is raw and powerful and certainly grabbing. I am speaking about a very bright AHHHHH type of sound. Think of Jerry Lewis yelling, " Laaaddddyyyy!" (if you remember Jerry Lewis) with that bright, spread child's voice. That is the type of 'color' that Broadway singing embraces. That type of color requires a singer to expose the voice and remove the safeguards for healthy technique. It requires the singer to disconnect from their lower support system and to sing entirely from the neck and the head. We will discuss this type of technique as we move forward in this book.

Think of your body as a large suspension bridge, much like the Brooklyn Bridge in NY. Sunk down in the ground on either side of the bridge are gigantic slabs of concrete which are connected to the cables which 'suspend' themselves over the length of the bridge. The sunken slabs of concrete pull the cables and create tension between the two sides of the bridge. They 'support' the part of the bridge which is carrying the weight of cars and trucks as they pass over. These slabs of concrete are the main support of the bridge but there are many other sources of support such as steel beams and wires and screws and bolts and more concrete along the length of the bridge.

Now, if somehow the cables connecting the two large sunken slabs of concrete were to be cut, the bridge would not automatically fall into the river. No, the bridge would still have support systems that would keep it up. The pressure of the cars and trucks passing over the bridge would be transferred from the sunken slabs and the large cables to secondary anchors like the steel beams and the wires and the screws and bolts.

Unfortunately the steel beams and wires and screws and bolts are not strong enough to keep the bridge up for as long a time as the sunken slabs of concrete were. Eventually the tension and pressure of all that weight crossing the bridge would eventually loosen the screws, bend the steel beams, loosen the wires and break the bolts. Slowly, maybe over a year or less, the bridge would start to become unstable. Parts of it might shake. Parts of it might swing back and forth. Pieces of the bridge might start breaking off.

Inevitably, one day, that bridge, after much trauma and damage, would collapse.

This is a metaphor for your voice. The sunken slabs of concrete are your lower diaphragm. The muscles of your abdomen and the muscles which allow you to do 'squats' and control your urinating and your anal sphincter are connected to your voice. Everything south of your belly button behaves just like the concrete slabs bearing the weight of your vocal gymnastics. If you cut off your lower body then the tension and pressure of singing is now put on the lesser muscles, like the screws and bolts and steel beams and wires of the bridge. The transitional period between loss of support and total collapse of the voice would include a wobbling tone and much hoarseness and laryngitis. Even worse, if you sing only from the neck and head, it is like removing the steel beams and wires and singing only on the screws and bolts. Very dangerous. But this is what singing Broadway asks a singer to do.

To a much lesser degree pop, rock and heavy metal singing ask less of the vocal apparatus unless, of course, the voice is being used in an industrial way day after day and week after week in stadiums and large venues. As I stated before singing these types of music can be damaging but the factors involved in lessening dangerous singing habits are at play. First of all the use of the microphone reduces the volume needed to be produced by the singer. The tailoring of the songwriting to the voice conceals vocal flaws. Also a lack of immediate exposure lessens the amount of time a pop singer will be in front of an audience. Many pop singers let the record speak for them and do not sing the songs repeatedly on the stage. Many types of pop singing involve nothing more than glorified speaking on pitch and require little diaphragm support or breath control. Some of the female artists sing like little children with tiny voices into the microphone. They become identified with this tiny little baby sound and never really use their voices to sing sustained high notes or difficult melodies. There are also many men or boys who sing with a little boy voice, barely above a whisper, who never really activate their diaphragm at all to increase volume.

Beyond these parameters there are also many performers who only lip sync to recorded tracks while in front of an audience. This may sound cheap and unprofessional but when you have a vast audience that is ignorant to the difference between a recorded voice and a live one and who really do not care one way or the other it is easy to see why the agents and technicians prefer to show off the singer this way. Live singing can only open the door to mistakes and mistakes are not allowed.

Another pitfall of live performance is the comparison to the recorded tracks that the audience is used to hearing. If the performer does not sound like they do in the recording the customer may not like it. What better way to give the customer the exact same vocal performance than to use a recorded track and have the performer lip sync to it?

This effort to perform songs live leads to various miscues and embarrassing moments for some singers. Because the majority of their experience is in the recording studio they are sometimes out of their element when singing into a microphone in front of a live audience in an acoustic environment. There is audio feedback. There is a certain amount of pitch correction to be taken into a account. They also need to have the music memorized. They have to be ready in case the song is mistakenly played in the wrong key...either too high or too low. They have to be ready to sing the entire song at one time because they do not have the luxury of stopping to collect themselves as they do in the studio when recording. So many factors go into reproducing a hit song when it's live and in front of an audience that it is no mystery why mistakes and bloopers happen.

Rock and heavy metal music present a more damaging type of singing than regular pop music. There is less actual singing and more shouting and yelling. I know voice teachers that make a lot of money showing rock singers how to shout and yell in a way that is less damaging to the voice. I'm serious. It is part of the business. If you are a parent with a teenager who is yelling and screaming rock or heavy metal or punk music let them know that they can do it and also learn how to reduce the amount of sore throats and laryngitis they will inevitably get by simply learning how to shape their vowels and control their volume.

One of the final types of singing styles is jazz. Jazz is a very complex and sensitive type of singing. It bridges the gap between classical and pop and Broadway. It has the beauty and complexity of classical singing mixed with the immediacy and modernity of pop music along with the style of Broadway. It takes quite a singer to pull off singing jazz. Many classical singers, because of their advanced technical training, try to 'cross over' to singing jazz but I am sure jazz lovers do not appreciate it. It takes a special voice and a special singer to sing jazz. There is an intimacy and a truthfulness to jazz that is required which goes beyond what singers do in pop or Broadway or even the classical style of singing. Jazz singers have to sound 'real'. Some of the most egregious and ugly types of singing are those when overbearing classical singers try to graft their opera technique onto jazz songs. It is pretentious and arrogant of them to think they can translate one type of technique to the other. Some, but very few, can do it and sound authentic. Songs like Summertime have been butchered by opera singers for decades. I am not an expert on jazz music or jazz singing, in particular, although the vocal apparatus works the same way for all types of singing. I do know that there are songs in the jazz medium that are best left to jazz singers alone. Pop singers also frequently try to sing jazz standards but they usually do not have the chops for it or their voices sound small and timid when trying. This also occurs when pop singers try to sing classical works. Because they are not connected to their body support below the neck or upper chest they do not have the power to raise the voice and to produce volume or to control the explosion of singing high notes or holding notes for long periods of time. The best strategy for these breathy, shallow singers is to sing even more softly to hide their flaws or to use a microphone. Watch the performances of Nicole Kidman in Moulin Rouge or Emma Stone and Ryan Gosling in La La Land to hear what I am talking about.

The last category, of course, is classical singing or opera which is my specialty. Thus, I will not spend a lot of time discussing it in this first book on Starting to Sing. Suffice it to say that this category presents some the most difficult music that can be sung by the human voice. This means that the amount of study and practice it takes to sing some of the repertoire is extensive. Learning classical music can lay the foundation for singing all the other types of music but does not guarantee that you will be good at them.

The strange thing about singing is that some of it seems preordained. I really wanted to be a blue eyed soul singer but my voice simply was not made for that. I am now singing, as a bass in opera, exactly what my voice is built to sing. It is true that I can cross over and sing some pop or jazz or Broadway but my first best destiny in singing opera. You may find that you or your child may want to sing some style in particular but that it simply does not suit your vocal mechanism. You just don't 'sound right' singing it. This should tell you something. So much sadness and misery have occurred because of people who stubbornly hold on to their 'dream' of what they want to do. No, I don't want to take away your dream but I want to let you know that some dreams can come true and some cannot. Understanding exactly what type of singer you are best designed to be and what your voice is capable of is the most important step in the development of a singer and I want to help you discover those truths.

Chapter 5

The Basic Basics

Over the years I have been increasingly less and less surprised by the appalling lack of knowledge most people have about singing and the mechanism of the voice. Even things that, on the surface, one would know or understand without a prior explanation they do not know.

I have already explained the most basic mechanical workings of the voice but there are other very basic concepts and facts that need to be understood by parents, children and adult singers that will definitely help them navigate the choppy waters of the music industry.

One of these concepts is that women sing higher than men. You would think that this was obvious information but, as I have seen, many people do not even understand this most basic fact. Women have smaller and shorter cords than men so their voices vibrate at a higher frequency. Children also sing higher than men, both little girls and little boys, because of the same reason.

When children go through puberty they experience a rapid growth phase which drastically changes the voice and makes it lower. Bigger longer cords translate into lower notes. A grown woman will have cords that are longer and thicker than the cords of a child. A young boy who goes thru puberty may have a drastic change of voice speedily progressing from a 'boy soprano' to a tenor, baritone or bass within a few short months. A little girl can remain a soprano as she passes through puberty but the voice will take on a more mature and fuller quality. Some little girls may have a drastic change like a boy soprano changing into a bass. These girls become 'altos' or 'mezzo-sopranos' which mean their high voices are lower than a soprano. Still, these lower voiced females have higher voices than most men. Certain high tenors or 'counter tenors' may have higher voices. These are exceptions and rare and we will not deal with them in this book.

All this is to say that you, as a parent or a singer, need to know that children have voices that change and they can only change in certain ways. A girl will never change into a full bass and a boy will never change into a high soprano voice. A little more than one hundred years ago certain organizations would castrate boy sopranos which prevented their testosterone from changing the voice through puberty and they would retain a soprano quality into their adult years (they were called 'castrati'). Thankfully this process is not popular anymore.

The reason this is important leads me to another basic idea which, to my surprise, is not so basic. This idea is that not every voice can sing every note on every piece of music. You would be surprised at how many times someone has come to me with a piece of music written for a soprano and expected me, as a bass, to be able to sing it. They figure that if you are a professional singer than you should be able to sing everything. Not true. My cords can only sing from the bottom of my range to the top of my range. Not the range of a soprano but the range of a bass. This is the same for tenors, baritones and mezzo-sopranos (altos).

In order of the highest voice to the lowest we list them as: Soprano, Mezzo-Soprano, Tenor, Baritone and Bass. There are subtle subdivisions of each of these voice categories but the most basic breakdown are those five categories. A bass can sing a little higher into the baritone range, a baritone can sing a little higher into the tenor range, a tenor can sing a little higher into the mezzo-soprano range and a mezzo can sing a little higher into the soprano range and vice versa when each of them tries to sing lower. This means the vocal ranges overlap but do not share a large part of the singable notes of each other.

So, if you are looking for a singer to sing a song at your wedding do not expect them to be able to sing any and all songs you give to them. They may be able to transpose or bring the key up or down to suit their range but, chances are, the song was meant for a different voice category and will sound different than you may be used to hearing when they sing it.

This concept can be applied to pop music or jazz singing or Broadway as well. Frequently a child or an adult singer will hear a song on the radio and try to sing along with it. They may find that it is too high for them and will start screeching and screaming and yelling in order to hit the high notes. They aren't able to sing the song not because they can't sing. They aren't able to sing the song because it is probably too high or out of their vocal range. This is such a basic idea but many people do not know it or understand it.

Thus, when a parent or friend hears the person

trying and failing, they are told to 'give it up' or admit that they can't sing instead of being encouraged to find out why they are not able to sing that particular song. Any song can be moved up or down in order to accommodate a singer. As long as the gender of the song fits (you don't want a man professing his love for another man unless the singer is supposed to be gay!) then you can change the 'key' of the song so that the person you want to sing it is able to.

Believe it or not I have also been approached to sing songs for an event where the singing 'character' is a female and speaks about loving a man. I do not understand why someone thinks this works.

Another very basic truth about singing, which many people do not think about, is that singers generally do not want to sing early in the morning and should not be pressed to do so if they do not want to.

The voice is part of your body. It responds like any other part of your body. It needs time to wake up. You don't jump out of bed and jog 20 miles an hour. You loosen up, you take a shower, you eat something and drink something. You concentrate or meditate and you prepare yourself for your day. The voice needs the same consideration.

By the same token the voice needs a healthy dose of sleep to function. I tell people I am a professional singer and a professional sleeper. I do whatever is necessary to get as much sleep as possible before I am supposed to sing. Obviously the more sleep you get the better the voice will work. Your body is a machine and so is your voice. These machines work best with healthy food, water and sleep. Sleep is frequently the forgotten factor when a voice begins to fade, get laryngitis or cracks.

One of the only things that forces me to cancel an audition is if I do not get enough sleep. Nothing can destabilize and weaken my voice as much as lost sleep. I am sure this is true for all different types of singing especially the types of singing that abuse the voice and force it to call for more rest in order to heal.

I guess the most insulting and ignorant presumption a singing neophyte or a regular everyday person can make is that all singers are the same. They think that any singer can sing anything and do not understand why that is not so when they ask you to perform something.

All people need to realize that every singer is unique and has special abilities that exist within specific parameters and they need to find out what those parameters are before making unrealistic demands. The same is true for parents who ignorantly run with their uneducated presumptions about their child and make decisions for them based on nothing but popular knowledge or their own emotional desires.

Another basic belief among people who are not educated about singing is that you have to be 'blessed' or born with the ability to sing and that if you are not it cannot be taught. This is wrong. Just because someone hits wrong tones when trying to sing and is inaccurate does not mean they do not have the ability. It simply means they are not focused or concentrating on what they need to do in order to produce the correct tone. I do not believe in the concept of 'tone deafness'. No one, except someone with a physical auditory deformity such as a defective eardrum, is tone deaf. Their brain may be tone deaf, but their ears are not. A 'tone deaf' brain can be recalibrated, exercised and taught to hear correctly. It is not easy and it takes time but it is not impossible.

I taught children at the John Robert Powers Talent Agency in New Jersey a number of years ago. I was frequently paid to teach multiple lessons to little boys and girls who had varied abilities in the singing department. One time I worked with a small boy who was about 7 years old. I would play a tone on the piano and he would ignore me and look around the room and then sing the wrong tone back to me. I told him to focus and listen and he continued to ignore me and sang the tone incorrectly again. Then I clapped my hands and snapped my fingers and told him strongly to listen and I played the tone again. This time he sang it correctly. Why? Because he thought about it first and focused. It is same idea hitting a target with a gun. If you blindly shoot you rarely will hit the target but if you focus and concentrate and aim the gun your chances of hitting that target will increase greatly.

What I learned from this experience was that the boy was not 'tone deaf'. He was 'tone indifferent'. He didn't care and he didn't know how to focus and tune into the note I was playing. Once I startled him and pushed him a bit he focused enough to actually pay attention to the note and he sang it back to me. Many people probably have the same issue. They are not paying attention. They are thinking about the weather or what they are going to eat for dinner. Once they focus and think about the tone they will most likely hit it.

From my observations the lag time between hearing a tone and being able to reproduce it correctly is a good gauge in judging how deep into the ballpark a potential singer is. Generally, if it takes 20 minutes to get someone to match a tone, they probably are not going to be a singer. Usually someone who really has the talent and wants to sing will respond quickly and pick up on what their teacher is looking for. If finding the right response is like pulling teeth it would not be surprising if the student does not go far as a singer.

Like many talents it is common for a young person to exhibit basic abilities and even advanced abilities early on. Some people just go there...they have a natural affinity for playing tennis or chess or lacrosse and they love it and they excel because of their love for it. These kids are a teacher's dream.

I am not saying that there aren't surprises with some students who, on the surface, look like they will never sing and then, one day, something happens and they start to bloom. This can never be discounted as a possibility. But, most of the time, the first blush reaction to how a child or adult sings when you start teaching them is the reaction that is ultimately proven right. Hard workers who become late bloomers are the exception to the rule.

Another popular belief among some people is that singing is easy. This one drives me crazy. I suppose many people want to believe that singing is easy so that they can explain why they do not sing and others do. In their minds they COULD sing IF they wanted to, since it is so easy to do. They just choose not to. Other people diminuate the

54

amount of effort it takes to sing because they cannot fathom the time spent doing exercises and learning rhythms and studying languages and particular styles of singing. It seems like a monumental amount of work and it is.

This type of ignorance is common among many people who discount intellect. They are most likely defensive about those with intellect and intelligence so they discount the disciplines such people master. People frequently say the same thing about mathematicians and physicists and writers and philosophers. It must be easy to do because I could do it if I tried, they think. Such arrogance.

No, unfortunately for these jealous and bitter individuals, there are actually abilities and disciplines that they CANNOT do and they simply can't admit it. Ego generates this response to singers and others who display a sharp ability for an intellectual discipline. I have heard some people say, " He became a singer because it was the simplest and easiest career path for him to take. " Such nonsense. It is a hard career and one that does not make for an easy life for most of those who choose it.

Someone that I know tried to explain my career choice as one where I get to be lazy, live a life of hedonism and glamour and never have to face 'real life' like most people do. I wish it were so. Singing as a professional opera performer is not really glamourous. You are only on stage between 20 to 60 nights a year, with an average career, and that is the most glamourous part of singing. Other than being on stage for those handful of nights you are staying in hotels and homes for weeks on end, you are on flights and trains and driving here and there all year long. You stay away from excessive partying and drinking in order to keep your voice in top form. No one really recognizes you when you leave the theatre because most opera singers are not famous. The pay is a pittance compared to pop singers or even Broadway. Only a select few get into the upper 5% that makes the big bucks. There is a constant worry about where the next job will be, how much the next contract will be for and why one contract was denied while another one was granted. Agents take money from you, the IRS takes money from you and you are an Independant Contractor which means, most likely, that you have no pension and no retirement. You might not even be able to get healthcare although Obamacare made that a bit easier in the USA.

I hate to paint a dire picture of being a singer but it is not the roses and glory that most people believe it is. If you do it you must have a strong love for the singing. If you sing just for money the lifestyle will kick you in the ass sooner rather than later. I know that for sure.

Chapter 6

We All Need Support

Deep breath is one large part of producing sound as an air converter. Another major component is support or using the 'diaphragm'.

Many people do not understand what or where the diaphragm is. If you are a shallow breather you probably do not have a decent connection to your diaphragm and, to sing correctly, you will need to work to establish a connection that is serviceable.

When I taught children at The John Robert Powers Talent Agency I was always amused when a child would be yelling and screaming in the hallway outside of my room and then, upon entering the 'singing zone', they would clam up and barely sing above a whisper. What happened?

The connection to the diaphragm is a mysterious one. Because it is all inside your body it can be hard to tell whether you are connected to it or not and sometimes it is not clear what the feeling of being connected is. After years of working on my personal connection to the diaphragm I have some advice and observations to make about it.

I was very thin when I began working to solidify the relationship between my voice and my diaphragm. I could not feel any observable difference between what I thought was an engagement of my lower body and the sound I was producing. I had learned to project my voice in a firm and strong fashion when I was a choir boy as well as in my high school choir and when I was in college. Until I attended to Academy of Vocal Arts in Philadelphia I never really actively did any exercise to find, relate to or access my diaphragm.

I realized, as I began taking voice lessons at AVA, that my connection was there but that I had no control over it and that it needed to be strengthened. But how?

I had learned how to do squats at the gym on a machine. I knew that was related. I also knew that the sphincter muscles connected to the anus and the 'pee muscle', which can voluntarily prevent someone from urinating in their pants, also played a role in this effort.

Over time I began to feel out where my diaphragm was and how it was having an effect on my singing. I would squat on my haunches on the floor and take a deep breath, very quickly, to cause my body to bounce. Another good exercise to connect to the diaphragm is to imitate monkey sounds. The OOH OOH of the monkey dips all the way down to the bottom of the system and gets a push from the diaphragm.

The most powerful way to connect to the diaphragm is to take notice of those instances where you generate volume without thinking. Think of when you have had to yell out loud in an emergency. Think of when you have needed to shout across the room or across the street to be heard. What if someone were about to be hit by a car and they weren't looking? How would you warn them without a microphone in your hand? You would have to yell! Engaging the muscles that are strong enough to allow your yell to be heard a long distance is engaging the diaphragm. The difference between yelling and singing is a difference of using blunt force and using finesse.

A dog does not think about barking. It does not prepare itself to bark. It simply barks. It can be heard down the street because it is naturally connected to its' diaphragm.

Human beings are similar in that, when they are jarred into activating the diaphragm because of an emergency, they produce a loud, supported sound with their voices.

A person who generates a limp, feeble sound when trying to sing is not connecting to any of those muscles and they are separated from their support and diaphragm. This does not mean that they are permanently damaged. It only means that they must work to establish a connection to activate those muscles.

Many times I have worked with a student who has shallow breathing and a dysfunctional connection to their diaphragm. In most of these cases the student, when asked, admits that they do not play sports or engage in any strong physical activities. You cannot be a singer without using your body and stressing your body.

For children I would recommend getting outside and playing some ball. Football, basketball, baseball...anything to get the child running and sweating and firmly manipulating an object. Swimming is also a wonderful activity. These sports will serve to connect them to their diaphragm and they will make them healthier in the bigger picture. Singing is not a physically effortless act. I frequently sweat and find myself out of breath, at times, while performing a role on the stage and singing. A physically involving role in an opera can be much like playing a game of racquetball. If you approach singing like an activity only done by the head and not the rest of the body you will never truly access the muscles and deep breathing necessary to sing correctly.

This approach indicates that singing is not only the generation of beautiful sounds with music but also primal and animal sounds. The two are related. Monkey sounds, dog barks, bird calls and any other type of primal hoot and scream will trigger a connection to the diaphragm which will, in turn, feed the volume of a sung tone because of the strengthened connection to the base and core of the body.

If you cannot force yourself to do some physical activity or make some monkey sounds or yell a bit then your connection to your diaphragm is going to be shallow at best because you will not repeatedly be exposing yourself to what makes your voice strong and full. Breath is not enough...you need power and power comes from the diaphragm.

Chapter 7

The True Voice

Leonardo da Vinci was asked once how he sculpted so beautifully. He responded, " This is simple. I just remove the rock from around the sculpture."

In much the same way this is what we are doing when we start to learn how to sing. Voice lessons and exercises and vocalises are repeated over and over again in order to 'remove the rock' from around the voice. We are, in the most simplest terms, rediscovering the 'true voice' when we work hard to become good singers.

Most of the time singing with a 'false voice' is what people find unpleasant when hearing a person singing. This means that they are 'putting on' a sound or 'affecting' a sound. An affected sound is a sound which is created by the voice which contains a purposeful distortion of the vibration of the sound the vocal cords make as the air passes through them.

This is most often accomplished by generating laryngeal pressure or distorting the mouth or face to alter the sound. Why would someone do this? Sometimes they are not doing it on purpose. They simply do not know how to generate a true and natural sound. They believe that distorting the voice, as they are able, to sound like some other voice they have heard is the best way to be a singer.

This is common with young kids imitating singing

they hear on the radio. They imitate a pop star as best they can by distorting the way they sing a vowel or a consonant. They put a twang in their voice or some other false affectation that is identified with the singer they are mimicking. It is very difficult to sound like yourself when you are trying to sound like someone else.

Now what do I mean by 'sound like yourself'? Understanding what that means is the key to learning how to sing correctly for people of all ages.

Your face is basically a stereo speaker. What I mean is that the sound of the vocal cords as air passes through them is magnified and 'broadcast' out of your face. The way your face is structured...the bone, the cheeks, the nose, the forehead and the combination of all of those creates a unique sound that is your voice and your voice alone.

You may have seen these crime detective shows where the police have a sample of someone speaking on the telephone who has committed a crime and they take the sample to a laboratory and they pass it through a recording device and then analyze it with a computer. What is generated is a graph of squiggly lines. That graph displays the 'fingerprint' of your voice. Virtually no one else has another voice like yours. Even if someone were to try to copy your voice, like an impersonator, the forensic investigation of the sound waves which make up the impersonators voice would, inevitably, fail to match the squiggly lines of the person they were trying to mimic.

This is because the bones and flesh of the face create a 'filter' through which the sound waves pass which are unique to one person and one person only.

In applying this to singing one can easily see the

correlation. The sound of your singing voice is shaped by the flesh and bone of your head and face and nothing can make you sound exactly like someone else. A truly unique and original singing voice is one that allows this fingerprint, this true voice, to live and breath. Putting on fake sounds and affecting a fake sound will never reveal your true voice.

One of the reasons why someone would put on a voice or fake one is because they are afraid of hearing their true sound. Much like someone who hates to hear their recorded voice speaking they are uncomfortable with what they hear and interpret the sound to be 'bad'. This is a person with low self esteem. Someone like this will find it very hard to sing because they do not think highly of themselves and do not have the motivation to reach out and manifest the liberation that is derived from singing. Singing is a powerful statement of the self and of the individual. If you are struggling to find that inner self and have a low opinion of yourself then singing will be a painful exercise in negative feedback.

Commonly people will mimic an opera singer, in a bad way, when they want to display some sort of 'singing' on their part. They will generate an exaggerated and bloated sound which is a caricature of the kind of beautiful sound a real opera singer makes. This is done to be funny, most of the time. Rarely does the person who mimics an opera singer, incorrectly, try to sing naturally and with their real voice. Usually this is because they have no confidence that their voice could possibly make such a lovely sound and they don't want to admit that so they make fun of it.

This does a disservice to opera singing and singing

in general. It creates a stereotype of classically trained voices which is unflattering and off-putting. It is no wonder that these art forms have begun to pass out of the popular consciousness when they are parodied and turned into gross misrepresentations of the real thing.

Similarly, good pop singers and jazz singers are also poorly imitated by novice singers who know of no other way to try to sing. I guess that trying to sing in these ways is better than not trying to sing at all but, at some point, a singer needs to realize that mimicking a popular star is only the first baby step towards learning how to sing correctly.

The real first step towards learning how to sing with YOUR OWN voice is to disassemble the voice and then reassemble it step by step. One of the hardest parts of teaching someone to sing is to get them to take it slowly. Everyone wants to reach third base in a day. It doesn't work that way. You cannot build a muscle in one day and you cannot become a good singer in one day. It takes time to get a feel for the mechanism, to get a feel for the breath and to understand and feel how the diaphragm is supporting your sound and how to work it.

Obviously many popular singers never even get that far. They have no idea how their diaphragm works, they have no relationship with their breath and they approach hitting notes like swinging an ax at a tree. This is the type of singer that will have a short shelf life and bow out of the game with nodes and operations within a few years.

Disassembling the voice means that they break the voice down to the simplest and most basic unit. I call that unit THE MOLECULE. A molecule in biology is one of the smallest building blocks of all matter. Two atoms of hydrogen and one atom of oxygen make up a molecule of water. If you are singing there are chains of oscillations that make up the sound wave which is your voice. Each oscillation could be called a 'molecule' of sound. If you can generate each individual oscillation or 'molecule' of sound correctly then you would be chaining together a long stream of 'perfect molecules' which, in turn, become long tones and phrases of music which is as pure and as 'perfect' sounding as human biology allows.

Now I am making this sound awfully complicated but it is really as simple as converting air into sound and paying attention to the process which aids in that conversion.

Breath out air. Exhale. Then inhale. Notice that very little sound is being generated. Certainly no music or tones are being made. Inhale again and now bring the cords together or, simply put, start making a 'sound'. It can be AH or OH or OOH. Whatever you like. At some point the air stops flowing and a sound is made, whether it is gruntlike or animalistic sounding is beside the point. This is the 'moment of conception' when air is utilized by the bringing together of the vocal cords to make sound. The sound is not pretty, it is primal. Getting in touch with these most primal sounds are very important in building the foundation of a good singing voice. You are playing with the most basic material.

Scientists frequently try to get samples of moon dust and to test dust from comets and meteors. Why? Because these dust particles are the stuff which makes up the trees and flowers and each of us. This dust is the primal material of the universe. In the same way the grunts and hoots and groans of the primal human voice are the basic building blocks of the singing voice of a pop star or an operatic tenor.

As you may notice the singing of an actual song is miles away from where we are starting. Why sing a song incorrectly and in a bad way when you could be spending your time fixing the core of your voice so that you are singing that song from the right place to begin with? I would rather have my students sing AH and OH and OOH for many weeks and have them feel the breath and the support and the proper genesis of their sound than have them sing SUMMERTIME or SOMEWHERE OVER THE RAINBOW over and over again incorrectly. Where is the productivity of repeating something wrong repeatedly?

Sometimes children who are trying to learn a song for a competition and have trouble with a high note or part of a phrase will repeat the song over and over again, ad nauseum, trying to fix it. Rarely does it work. Why? Because they are not dealing with the core reason they are cracking or thinning out on top. They are simply repeating the incorrect approach to the note or phrase over and over again.

What needs to happen is that the singer, preferably with a teacher, will take the phrase or note that is giving them trouble and deconstruct it. Sing the note on a different vowel. Try singing an octave below and rise to the note. Sing the phrase with a lip trill (blowing air thru closed lips) and a hum. Sing the entire phrase on one vowel leaving out the consonants. There are many different ways to approach these problems. Hopefully, after experimenting with the phrase, some kind of alteration of a vowel or strengthening of the breath support will allow the singer to finally conquer the troubled passage. Simply repeating the wrong approach will only lead to the same poor sound being generated over and over again.

When I teach a Masterclass I frequently will ask the singers to bring their worst phrase, their worst note or passage to work on. This is the meat and bones of becoming a better singer. You must conquer your fears and the only way to do that is to solve your technical problems head on. Once you isolate the note or word you are having a hard time with you can then start to approach it from different ways in order to find some answer and sing it well. Over time this strategy will work.

My goal, in this chapter, is to get the singer to realize that there is a way of singing that is better than another way. Finding your true sound is the most important step in becoming a singer that people want to hear. It is possible that you believe you are a good singer but you are actually 'putting on' a sound or affecting a sound that is not your own. The listener can tell the difference. There is a discernible acoustic flavor to a real and true sound and a fake, affected one. Start listening to your sound or the sound of your child singing and make the determination if they are singing with their 'real' voice or a fake one. This is one of the most basic steps in setting off on the correct path to vocal health while singing.

Chapter 8

Changing Those Vowels

So what makes singing certain words so hard for some singers? Well, the answer must be the way the singer is singing a specific vowel. Vowels make up 50% of what we sing. The other 50% are consonants. You can't have anything other than a vowel or a consonant be part of what is being sung because vowels and consonants are all we can form with our mouth, lips and tongue.

Sound can only really flow from a vowel. It is hard to make a K or a P or a B phonate. These are percussive consonants. Yes you can hum on an M or an N but that is not singing, it is humming. You can also whistle but we are not discussing that in this book.

One of the easiest and greatest kept technique secrets in singing is the use of 'vowel modification' to fix various singing problems for the novice and even for advanced singers. A vowel is a not a static, constant or fixed sound. There are variations of color for each vowel we form when we sing. If you go through every permutation of vowel color there is a vast array of colors starting with a closed E sound, through EH and AH and OH and OOH. The spaces in between each major vowel are the places where we craftily insert 'modifications' to make the singing of a word easier.

The biggest problem most new singers or untrained singers run into is that they try to literally sing the exact vowel of a word. This is foolish. When you sing in your midrange or around the pitch of your speaking voice you can do this. But when you start to sing higher pitches it becomes much harder to do. Why? Because the pressure created by closing the cords to sing a higher pitch is at odds with the forming of a natural open vowel. Singing AH on a high note is much harder than singing AH in your speaking range. AH will tend to shift to some form of UHH as you rise to higher pitches. This shift from AH to UHH elongates the mouth and the oral cavity allowing for the larynx to relax and the cords to vibrate more freely. The listener will not hear any discernible difference between AH and UHH when it is placed on a high note. I call this an 'acoustic illusion'.

The same can be said for singing AYY (a closed E) in the speaking range and then rising into a higher pitch and modifying the vowel to some sort of EHH (open E). In both the cases of AH to UHH and AYY to EHH there is a dropping of the jaw and a relaxation of the larynx as the voice attempts to sing a pitch on a closed vowel. We are opening the vowel a bit to let off pressure...like releasing the valve on a pressure cooker to let off steam before we open it.

What I am describing to you on these pages is worth the price you paid for this book. This vowel modification approach is pure gold and is something that most every halfway decent voice coach can get loads of mileage out of as they teach their students. I am letting you hear about for very little compensation. I must be crazy!

I am letting you in on these powerful techniques because I want you to understand how singing works and what must be done to create a great singer who is not going to harm themselves with bad choices. Vowel modification is the most basic tool in the bag of tricks for a voice teacher. Be wary of any voice teacher that does not practice, enforce or introduce vowel modification to their students. They probably don't know what they are doing.

The essence of what vowel modification does is to trick the voice into singing a word with a closed vowel on a high note by altering the vowel just enough to sing it with less pressure and just enough for it to still be understood as the same word to the listener.

For instance the word HARD can be sung with the AH of HARD exactly how you would say it in conversation when it is sung on notes within the normal speaking range of the singer. But when you try to sing HARD in the upper register it must be altered somewhat to a variation of the word somewhere between HARD and HURD...actually we would probably eliminate the R altogether when we go up into a high note because most R's are understood when they are in the middle of a word. This approach sort of 'Britishofies' the word but it works technically. Try singing HARD in your speaking range and then singing HUD on a high note. You will find that HUD is much easier to sing on the high note and eliminating the R makes it even easier and it can still be understood by the listener.

The word is easier to sing because singing HUD forces you to drop your jaw and creates more space for the phonation of the word. It also relieves pressure in the oral cavity because it is open more. Singing HARD literally up there would force you to bite down and close up the

STARTING TO SING BOOK 1

mouth and throat.

Singing a closed vowel is much easier up on the higher notes than singing an open vowel. Singing AYY or EEE up on a top note is far easier than singing AH or OH. This may seem to contradict what I just wrote about opening the mouth and relieving pressure but that is for singing open vowels on top. Open vowels need to shift to more open vowels. Closed vowels do not need to be opened to be sung up on top because they benefit from the pressure of singing a high note. This is very complicated to explain but stay with me.

Depending on where in your range a closed vowel is sung it could benefit from opening more or closing more. BREAK can turn into BRECK on a higher tone but then benefit from staying BREAK on an even higher tone. This has to do with placement and we will not delve into that too much here.

Placement creates the color of your sound. Singers can either sing with a forward placement, a middle placement or a back placement. When one begins singing the safest placement is to stay back. Eventually, as you get better and feel more confident, a teacher should show a student how to bring the placement forward a bit. Extreme forward placement and extreme back placement create sounds that are usually unpleasant to hear.

What I mean by back is back in the throat...which is a more dark and 'covered' sound. Forward means in the front of your mouth and is usually a bright sound. The perfect mix is a middle placement but this is not easily found right away so, to be safe, the singer is shown how to put the voice back so the sound is 'covered' and has a far

STARTING TO SING BOOK 1

less chance of 'cracking' or breaking than if it were forward.

Think of a lampshade or the lack of one. If a lightbulb is bare it is very hard to look at. Putting a shade over it still allows light to shine but not so much that you have to squint and look away. A bare bulb is stark and shocking. A covered bulb creates ambient light which you can read by and it can be looked at directly without discomfort.

Some voices are bare bulbs. They shine brightly and the sound is almost unbearable to hear. It is extremely forward. Like the WAHHHH of a baby which is probably the brightest and loudest sound you can hear.

An extremely bright sound is not a sound that brings much pleasure to the ear of a listener. Only when we muffle that sound a bit or bring it back...put some kind of shade on it...does it become palatable enough to be able to stand for extended periods of time. A moderate shade or cover of the voice entails bringing the sound backwards from the front of the mouth where the teeth are and into the space where the roof of the mouth creates a shell. This can be simulated by moving from a loud AHHHH to UHHHH. Forward and then back a bit. If you vascillate back and forth between AH and UH you will feel the placement move from forward to the middle and back again. This is the type of change that is needed when singing to change the placement of sound.

Now if you combine UH with OH the sound will move back even further, closer to the throat in the back of the mouth. This is a back placement. Try moving back and forth between UH and OH to see if you can feel the sound move from the middle of the mouth to the back of the mouth. This is a bit harder to do.

It may seem as though most of the techniques and tricks that I am discussing are meant to aid in the proper singing of words up on higher tones and this is because that is exactly right. Almost everything we do in teaching is aimed at aiding the student to sing high notes. Singing in the mid range and on the bottom are fairly straightforward as long as you have the proper placement. No matter whether high or low if you are singing too far forward it is not pleasant to hear. Singing too far forward on top is very destructive to the voice...even more so than in the middle or on the bottom. That is because the increased pressure batters the vocal cords more when singing a high note incorrectly.

Perhaps another good way of approaching high tones, other than vowel modification, is the simple idea that high and low really do not exist in singing. Why do we apply the idea of high and low to the notes of a scale? It seems quite unnecesary to me to look at a note that has a different pitch than another as either 'high' or 'low'. You are not reaching up for a box of cereal on the top shelf of the supermarket when you sing a high note. You are not reaching down onto the floor when you sing a low note. Why do we see these tones as high or low?

These notes are more accurately 'short' and 'long'. If we are being specific the correlation between creating a 'high' tone and singing a 'low' tone is that for high tones the cords are being stretched longer and for low tones the cords are becoming shorter. Think of a guitar string. When you twist the knob on the top of the guitar you are winding up the string to give it a higher pitch. You release the string to bring the pitch down. There is no high or low in direction. There is only longer and tighter or shorter and looser. Perhaps if we approach the voice from this perspective the singing of 'high notes' will change and we will be much calmer and not try to 'reach' a high note. Unfortunately when we look at a page of music the notes are written in a linear fashion and they are up or down on the staff and the notes that are higher on the page are higher in pitch. But, when applied to the physiology of the vocal mechanism, there is no up or down.

When singing a 'high note' a person should try to do everything possible to relax everything around the cords so that the tone can be phonated in a comfortable way. If the cords are tight and the neck is tight and the face constricts and the body braces itself how can the tone be anything but a catastrophe waiting to happen?

The visualization that should be embraced for singing a high tone is one that imagines the voice as being long, not high. Imagine a string coming out of your throat straight in front of you. When you are singing a high note someone is pulling the string. It is not rising higher it is merely getting longer and more firm. We do not want to say it is increasing in tension because tension is the last thing a singer should be thinking about. Firmness is a much better word and a much better concept to embrace when trying to sing a high note. It is hard not to use the word 'high' to describe what I am explaining because the word and the idea of highness and lowness have become so firmly ingrained in the academia and teaching of singing that we can hardly get away from it.

It is best to try to reject the idea of singing high or low and simply try to sing a firm tone or a loose tone. They have no direction. High tones are firm, low tones are loose (even though there is a firmness about every tone that is sung correctly).

So, accepting that we are not singing high or low but either singing firmly or loosely, the degree to which we apply vowel modification is clear in how we relieve tension when the cords are pulled forward and made firmer. If they become too tight then they 'snap together' or 'crack'. It is a delicate balance to sing firmly and yet not so firm that you crack. Preventing cracking is where vowel modification comes in.

If you sing a vowel and it goes beyond the pressure point where the cords can vibrate comfortably they snap open and you crack. To keep them closed you need to put a 'lampshade' over them and modify your vowel so it is a bit darker and rounder than the actual spoken vowel. TAKE morphs into TECK and the word HATE morphs into the word HET.

Another piece of this modification puzzle is what is called a 'dipthong'. I could write a whole other chapter on dipthongs but I really didn't want to name a chapter 'dipthongs' because it would look pretty funny so I am including them in the chapter on vowel modification.

Dipthongs and the presence of syllables make up a vast amount of singing technique and we will discuss it here. Dipthongs are vowels that transition from the front of the mouth to the back of the mouth. When you say BREAK you are actually speaking an open EH vowel in the front of your mouth before you end the word with an EE in the back of your mouth. We can dissect the word into syllables to see what is happening.

Normally an english teacher would say that the word BREAK is ONE SYLLABLE. One beat...quickly said is BREAK. But, to a singer, there is a much bigger pallette of sounds contained within a short word like BREAK. A singer can take that word and stretch it out into BUH-UR-AY-EEK. Those are four singing syllables.

We can do this with all words. The word TREMBLE would normally be seen as having two syllables...TREM-BULL. But for a singer the word becomes TUH-UR-EMM-BULL with four syllables. Why? Because the vowels create spaces between the consonants that must be sung. You can speak a word quickly when you are talking to someone two feet in front of you but when you are trying to make a word understood to 2,000 people from 100 yards away you need to annunciate the words better and with more specificity.

The word GREAT would be seen as a one syllable word to most people. But when we sing it the word is stretched out and becomes GUH-ERR-AY-EET. Four syllables.

Look at words as being made of rubber and when you stretch them out spaces form between consonants like the space between your fingers when you splay them open. You have to sing the consonants AND the spaces. If you don't the words you sing will be far less understandable to the audience. Really, the way you treat vowels and consonants is the difference between singing and speaking.

So, when coupling the stretching of words to create

more sung syllables, you also take into account the movement of an open vowel to a closed one in the creation of dipthongs. GREAT and BREAK both contain dipthongs. The words begin on an open vowel, GREH and BREH and then they begin to move backwards towards EET and EEK. Of course how many syllables you are able to stretch and open up and sing depends on the length of the note you are given to sing the word on. If I have lots of time I can sing GUH-UR-AYY-EET. But if I have a short note I might have to collapse the word a bit and sing GREH-EET or BREH-EEK. One way or the other the journey of the word is from the front of the mouth to the back of the mouth. So, why is this important?

The pitfall of many singers is that they do not know there is a dipthong occuring and they sing in a midway position closing towards the dipthong. If we are searching for the least amount of tension in a word when we are singing it we want to sing the most open and relaxed vowel. So we would sing GREHHHHHHHHHH and then, at the last second, go to EET. We would not want to sing in the middle of the transition between GREH and EET. That middle area is an area of tension and it is a muddled vowel that is neither EH or EE. So when singing BREAK I would sing BREHHHHHHHH and then when the note is over tack on EEK. Listen to some of your favorite pop songs when the vocalist sings a high note and, if they are good, they will sing a high (firm) tone with the open forward vowel of the word held in the beginning and the dipthong (closed and tighter vowel) tacked onto the end of the note. This makes for a less tense and more comfortable phonation of the word.

There are other hidden vowels and syllables and consonants among many of the words that are sung in any given song or aria. One of the most unnoticed 'shadow vowels' that appear are the ones that exist in the formation of a word. Some words have a consonant as their first letter and we assume that we are going to sing that word from a dead start. Take the word WHERE for instance.

Is there a vowel hidden in that word? Where could it be? Well, you could Britishify the word and sing WEHHH-UHHH without and R. But that is not what I am talking about.

Ok, the hidden vowel is an OOH vowel...as in the word MOO, like a cow does. If you pronounce the word WHERE slowly, before you form the W, there is an OOH that transforms itself into a W...as in OOH-WEHHH-UHHH. That OOH is SUNG as opposed to starting dead on a W and quickly singing WEH-UHH.

OOH-WHEN, OOH-WHY, OOH-WHAT. The transition into a word like WHAT is made much more musical by singing an OOH before the W.

Another hidden sound that accentuates the annunciation of sung words is the humming of an N or an M at the beginning of them. NNNNNNNNOTHING.....or MMMMMAYBE I WILL! Taking your time and being patient to tack on a hummed N or M for many words will make them more understandable to your audience and will keep the air flowing and moving instead of having dead starts.

The same can be done for L's at the beginning of words and even S's and R's and V's. You need to sing thru these phonated consonants with vibration and air. VVVVVVERY OOH-WELL or LLLLLLOVELY OOH-WUH-MUN. Also you can sing URRRRRREADY OR NNNNNOT. You can even start SSSSSINGIN IN THUH RRAIN.

Many coaches will find fault with this approach to singing because they have had it drilled into their heads that pronouncing a word correctly should take priority but they do not take into consideration that the words that are sung need to hit the back of the theatre. During a coaching the singer is five feet away and the exaggeration of these elongated vowels and consonants preceded by exaggerated vowels sound jarring and overdone. But, in a full hall of people with a populated back row balcony, your 'over' exaggeration is a Godsend to those audience members who actually want to understand the words that are being sung. Even if a singer uses a microphone this technique of elongating vowels and adding elongated vowels to certain consonants (plus elongated the voiced consonants) will be welcome and praised for the added annunciation that will appear.

SPECIAL SECTION
Guidelines and Advice

1. Soon after you or your child starts to sing, in whatever capacity, take the time to learn about the basics of what you are doing.

2. Every singer has a finite range of tones that they are able to sing. Every singer has an ultimate high note and an ultimate low note. Find out what these are for you or your child. Once you do this you will also know what your category is: soprano, mezzo, tenor, baritone or bass.

3. Be aware that you can alter the color of your voice by placing it backwards or forwards in the mouth and throat. Many times, when singing for the first time, the placement can be wrong and the vocal quality may be quite ugly until corrected. Forward placement will make the voice brighter and backward placement will make the voice darker.

4. Understand that not every singer can sing every song. Since every singer has a finite range they must sing songs which are written within that range or they will be screaming out high notes or mumbling low notes for which their voice is not suited.

5. Singing is about using the breath. If you do not breathe deeply you will not have the 'gas' to fuel the voice and you will sing shallow tones with no power.

6. A voice that is connected to deep breathing and a

lower part of the diaphragm will have more power and will be able to endure more industrial type singing.

7. Trying to sing exactly like another singer is a poor way to achieve success and is a strategy which can harm the voice permanently. One should always strive to sing with their 'real' voice.

8. Simply repeating parts of a song which are hard to sing is no way to fix the problems you may have. The difficulty must be dissected and fixed in order to finally sing something that is bothering you.

9. Altering vowels is the simplest and most effective way to ease the pressure of higher tones when the vowel being sung is too difficult. Because the tones usually sung with an altered vowel are higher tones the shift to a darker vowel is rarely noticed. Higher tones 'mask' the altered vowel.

10. There is no such thing as a high note or a low note. All notes are either 'firm' (or tight) or loose. Dispensing with the idea of a 'high note' will go a long way towards singing with reduced tension. When you approach a 'firm' tone do what you can to reduce the tension involved with singing it by dropping the jaw and slightly altering the vowel to be more open. The more 'loose' you are able to feel when singing low the better the voice will sound. In either firm or loose notes there is still a basic frame around the tone which maintains some amount of 'firmness'.

11. Good diction is a function of singing clear vowels between consonants and stretching out words like

rubber bands as you 'phonate' through them. Even the beginning of a word that starts with a consonant, like WHEN, begins with the vowel OOH which should be sung thoroughly before continuing on into the word OOH-WHEN.

12. Do not listen to non-professionals about the quality of your voice or the voice of your child. Also do not pass your own non-professional judgements about the potential of a particular voice. Get someone with credentials and a good track record of working with successful singers to assess a voice.

13. Understand that singing can be a cruel and difficult business for children and also adults. There are many ill-informed teachers, coaches and 'experts' who can lead you down a destructive path. There is no way to completely avoid these individuals but it helps to know that not everyone has the best interest of the singer at heart.

14. Industrial singing, for a child or adult who is 'discovered' and plugged into a formulaic professional career path, must find a way to get honest feedback from a voice professional and not get stuck 'in the bubble' of sycophantic handlers and executives who only wish to make a fortune off of a 'flash in the pan'. No one that invests in a child singer is really looking for a long term investment. Most of them want to have a short term cash cow and will abandon these children once they hit puberty and their voice changes or, even worse, are destroyed by poor technique and misguided vocal instruction.

15. It is important for every singer to know what KEY they are singing a song in and if the printed music you are providing for a pianist is in the KEY that is the most comfortable and appropriate for you to sing. Not every song is in a KEY you will be comfortable with. This is also true for singing The National Anthem at sporting events. Make sure you KNOW which key they will play the CD in and that the KEY is one that you are able to sing in. For every song there is a BEST KEY and that is the one you should indicate. The KEY will depend on your RANGE.

16. There is a big difference between a pre-recorded CD version of a song that a singer will sing to and a live accompanist who will play your song on a piano or synthesizer. A pre-recorded song will play at the same speed (tempo) every single time no matter what a singer does. The singer must MATCH the tempo of a pre-recorded CD song. An accompanist is able to judge the tempo that a singer is taking in a song and alter the way they play to match and help the singer succeed in singing the song. There is also more of a 'living' quality to a singer that sings with a live accompanist than a canned, dead and repetitive CD recording.

17. Using a microphone can be a blessing or a curse for many singers. A microphone can amplify a voice but a singer must also be able to create some kind of appreciable volume naturally without the microphone. Constantly relying on a microphone to amplify the voice will create a singer that has no

STARTING TO SING BOOK 1

connection to his diaphragm and will create a much more shallow connection to the body. If you cannot make your voice louder and softer without a microphone then using a microphone to do it is a cheap and harmful way to sing in the long run.

18. Many modern songs are not worth using as material to learn how to sing with. This is also true of many modern Broadway tunes. Most new pop songs or Broadway songs are not well written for the voice and will not present any kind of challenge to make a voice better. These songs 'talk down' to the voice and present it with extremely simple and rangeless non-melodies which will prevent the voice from being equipped to handle more melodic and complicated compositions.

19. A singer needs to drink enough water, get enough sleep and refrain from screaming, smoking, incessant talking or prolonged coughing. The cords are delicate pieces of flesh and they must be treated with respect.

20. Singing a song should be the final part of the process. Correctly learning to sing is not about repeating the song over and over again, mistakes and all. Correctly learning to sing means dissecting the problems and fixing them. One does not build muscles by playing tennis. One builds muscles by lifting weight so that one can play tennis. Singing vocalises (exercises on vowels) is like lifting weights and singing a song with words and rhythm is like playing tennis.

21. Most of the difficulty in singing lies with singing

words on higher (more firm) tones. Almost all of the techniques in a voice lesson revolve around this issue. Other major issues are correctly singing musical notation, singing on the breath and diaphragm, having proper diction and annunciation, singing in a foreign language and memorization.

22. A pure and natural or 'true' singing voice should be very close to the sound of the speaking voice. If you analyze your speaking voice and familiarize yourself with the sensation and 'feedback sound' of your speaking voice you should have the proper parameters with which to judge the 'true sound' of your singing voice. The only time that the quality of the singing voice should differ from the quality of your singing voice (except in the increased volume when singing) is when the singer sings a higher (firmer) tone. As the tones go 'up' the distortion of the color of the sound will diverge from the speaking voice. Still, maintaining a sound as close to speaking as possible when going 'up' is preferred.

23. One should practice some kind of simulation of starting the voice from nothing, to the beginning of sound and then to a full phonation on a random vowel of the individual's choice. This is the process of ONSET and is a valuable addition to the various techniques of singing properly.

Chapter 9

Onset

Perhaps we should have started this book with onset given that I believe it is one of the most important and vital techniques in singing properly. I decided not to start with it because it is a much more esoteric and misunderstood, if not unknown, part of learning how to sing.

When I was accepted to the Academy in Philadelphia back in 1996 I was mistakenly assigned to a different voice teacher than the one I had expected to be working with. I was assigned to the legendary Louis Quilico (1925-2000) who was a Canadian born baritone with a 25 year Metropolitan Opera track record and over 700 performances of Rigoletto.

Instead of objecting to the clerical mistake of putting me on Mr. Quilico's roster I went to Bill Schuman (whom I had expected to study with) and asked him if it might be ok to try working with Mr. Quilico for just a semester to see what he had to say and to impart on me whatever bits of technical knowledge he might have to give. Bill thought it was fine.

When I had my first lesson Mr. Quilico listened to me sing an aria and acknowledged that I had a fine voice. He then told me a story about his debut at the San

Francisco Opera when he was a very young man.

He told me that he was nervous about making his debut and that he was sure that he was not yet ready technically to sing in the proper way for such a prestigious company as San Francisco. They had put him in a small apartment and for days he sat there and concentrated on his technique. After awhile his concentration became meditation and he told me he had a revelation about what to do with his voice.

The revelation had to do with the air that was used to begin singing. He believed he was taking in the air incorrectly and not utilizing it efficiently. Although by this time he was already a magnificent singer with a budding career he was not content to sit on his laurels and stop his vocal education.

He told me that he sat in a chair and stared at the wall and thought about breathing and it's relation to singing. He made the intellectual observation that the voice had a beginning. It started from somewhere. He knew, of course, that the breath was part of this but other parts of the engagement of the voice were less clear.

He began to breath in and out and slowly engage the mechanism of the cords to 'phonate' or make a sound. This sound was not specifically a 'tone' or a 'note' of any kind but more accurately like a grunt. Mr. Quilico was playing with the edge of his voice and making himself aware of how the process of singing was generated.

From there he took the next most logical step. He went from breath to grunt to fully engaged singing on a vowel. This included long drawn out breaths with a slow transition from breath into a short grunt and then a normal singing tone. He realized that when one sings the length of time was much shorter between the breath and the 'phonated note' so he sped up the interval in which he was engaging the cords.

What he eventually perfected was a short, quick exercise that he continued to use for the remainder of his life and he imparted that exercise to his students. Some thought it was nonsense. Others, like myself, learned it and used it to make our voices better.

While doing the exercise one must listen closely to judge whether the sound is 'real' or fake and one must also take the time to become a critic of one's own voice to judge if it is being cleanly produced or a 'dirty' sound.

The exercise is, as he described it, a simulation. If we watch major sports figures playing their respective games we can see professional athletes who have perfected physical simulations which allow them to expedite winning moves within competitions they are participating in. A tennis player bounces the ball as they stand waiting to serve. They wish to serve an ace every time but that is not possible. They can perfect their serve to hit aces more than most people but this takes practice. If you watch a tennis match you will see the player bounce the ball, bounce the ball, bounce the ball and then, at some point, they commit to the action, their body tenses up, they throw the ball into the air and then their body becomes a sleek and graceful weapon that reaches up and hits the ball with power and grace.

Arriving at the point where you can serve an ace a majority of the time takes thousands of practice serves over years of time. The same is true of activating the voice to cleanly produce notes or tones that are centered and perfectly balanced. We must simulate the act of starting to sing.

This practice is defined as 'onset'. It is the practice of beginning to sing before the note is sounded. We sing before we sing. Our body is prepared to produce the tone seconds before we actually produce it. One may think this is such a simple and rudimentary concept that it hardly merits an exercise but I beg to differ. Each of us, when doing any activity of high skill, needs to practice and simulate that activity under adverse circumstances, compensating for variables and distractions.

If a singer learns to do this the frequency and reliability of the voice to produce nearly the same quality tone every single time the voice is used is increased exponentially. One sculpts and molds the voice into a shape that is repeated over and over again until the singer retires.

I discussed this approach earlier in the book when I spoke about THE MOLECULE. Using ONSET is what creates the desired molecule of perfected sound. I spoke about it before in context of revealing the TRUE VOICE. It is also integral in assuring that the true voice become uniform and reliable over long periods of time.

Once a quarterback learns how to throw a ball correctly, with all the nuance and specificity that is necessary to hurl the ball 10, 20, 30 or 60 yards for a score, then they have that skill for a lifetime. It becomes as simple and as easy as breathing. The repetitious exercises eventually get sublimated by the muscles in the body and you engage the air and cords with the same approach every

STARTING TO SING BOOK 1

single time you do it.

Much of the essence of this exercise is related to the Italian singing school of 'drink the sound'. They describe good singing as approaching phonation as if you are breathing IN instead of breathing OUT. The theory is that breathing in relaxes the throat and all the mechanisms of singing and puts them in the perfect position to sing relaxed firm tones. The problem is that, of course, humans cannot make a sound with the cords when breathing in. Air must pass over the cords going OUT in order to phonate. So, by simulating onset, we 'fool' the voice into operating with the feeling of an inhalation during the reality of an exhalation.

It sounds complicated and it is. But, like all physical processes, it can be learned and perfected by trusting the body and the muscle memory of the throat and vocal apparatus.

Mr. Quilico's onset exercise may be hard to figure out without actually hearing and seeing it in person but I will try to describe it as best I can here.

1. Hold one hand up at about face level with the palm face down. The hand may be limp and relaxed.
2. Without anyone else instructing you to do so pick a moment to drop your hand. This moment should be when you are 'ready' to do so.
3. As your hand falls take in a short but deep breath of air.
4. After your hand falls to about belly level sing a tone in your mid-range close to your speaking tone with

a vowel of your choice immediately without taking another breath.

5. Let your hand rise back up to where it started.

The essence of this exercise is to take a breath in and then, very quickly, sing without any further preparation in order to 'capture the moment' of the relaxation of the body during inhalation. It's a kind of trick but it works. You capture the moment, the match is lit, and you bottle it by singing. If you wait too long then the moment is stale and the rigidity of the vocal apparatus is reasserted. You need to capture the perfect moment of looseness and firmness during the breath.

This exercise is much more complicated than it looks and sounds on the surface. At first glance one might question whether it has any impact on the voice at all. But, I can tell you, after 25 years of singing and using this exercise, it has put an ease and a vitality into my singing that I would not have had without it. I do not think about singing or activating the voice. I just do it. There is no more thought given to singing than there is to breathing which is at it should be for a professional singer.

Onset gives a performer an extra added tool to insure vocal health and stability, to create a 'safe zone' around the voice and to make singing that much more pleasurable. A singer cannot spend a career 'lurching' into a phonated tone. Each tone must be a perfect jewel formed in the fire of proper breathing technique and lifelong repetition.

Closing Thoughts

My purpose in writing this book was to offer a basic, honest and informative assessment of the singing world and your participation in it. Included were various technical ideas to help along anyone who has already embarked on a singing journey.

It should be clear, after reading this book, that singing is not an easy business and that it is not for the faint of heart. Each person who commits to singing, or commits to helping their child to sing, is committing to something difficult, challenging and sometimes unachievable. Not everyone can succeed at singing which is why not everyone does.

My greatest hope for those who endeavour to sing professionally is that they do so with an eye on the health of their instrument. A washed up, used and abused voice is the saddest spectacle one can witness in the music world. Good vocal health stems from good vocal technique. Singers should always be on the lookout for tips and advice on how to sing in the most efficient and healthy manner.

Also, there is much more to be discussed and learned about singing than I have mentioned in this book. Here we have only grazed the surface and the most basic ideas concerning the implementation of voice technique. Do not take what is written in STARTING TO SING and leave it there. Go on and explore more literature, seek more advice and ask more questions. I will be following up this book with another one that tackles more specific issues and more difficult problems.

I wish you luck upon your adventure with singing and remember that if you take care of your voice it will always take care of you.

Valerian Ruminski
April 26th, 2017

ABOUT THE AUTHOR

Valerian Ruminski is a graduate of SUNY-Buffalo with a BA in Voice as well as an Artist Diploma from the prestigious Academy of Vocal Arts in Philadelphia. He made his Metropolitan Opera debut in 2001 as well as debuts at Carnegie Hall, Avery Fisher Hall and the NYC Opera. Mr. Ruminski has performed in opera companies around the world and has taught for the John Robert Powers Talent Agency as well as Westchester Community College in Valhalla NY. He is also the Founder of Nickel City Opera in Buffalo NY and has been the General Director since 2009.

www.valerianruminskibass.com

Made in the USA
Columbia, SC
16 December 2017